On Our Way with Jesus
A Journey of Christian Initiation

We Share in
the Eucharist
Preparation for First Communion

Francoise Darcy-Berube and John-Paul Berube

**When Jesus invites us to share
The Bread of Life from Heaven
He also invites us to share
The bread and riches of this earth.**

NOVALIS

ST. ANTHONY MESSENGER PRESS

CASSELL

Table of Contents

We Share in the Eucharist:
Preparation for First Communion

Authors: Francoise Darcy Berube and John Paul Berube

Editor: Patrick Gallagher

Production Consultant: Gaynor Fitzpatrick

Layout and design: Annie Pencrech

Illustrations: Hélène Bouliane: cover; Heather Collins: 10, 11, 12, 24, 39, 46, 51, 56, 61; Lucie Faniel: 8, 63; June Lawrason: 28, 29; Céline Malépart: 9, 27, 31, 36, 37, 47, 49, 50, 55, 58, 61; Caroline Merola: 3, 14, 26, 30, 35, 41, 42, 43, 44; Anna Payne-Krzyzanowski: 64; Georgette Pusztai: 4, 5, 6, 7, 13, 18, 19, 20, 21, 22, 23, 24, 29, 30, 32, 34, 38, 40, 44, 45, 46, 52, 53, 54, 55, 56, 57, 59, 60; Anne Villeneuve: 16, 17, 33

© 1997 Novalis, Saint Paul University, Ottawa, Canada

Imprimatur: Most Rev. Marcel Gervais, Archbishop of Ottawa, February 1997.

Business Office: Novalis Publishing, 49 Front Street East, 2nd Floor, Toronto, Ontario M5E 1B3, Canada.
Tel: 1-800-387-7164. Fax: (416) 363-9409.
E-mail: novalis@interlog.com

ISBN 2-89088-858-4

Printed in Canada

Distributed in Great Britain and Ireland by Geoffrey Chapman, an imprint of Cassell, Wellington House, 125 Strand, London WC2R OBB

1 We are invited to the Lord's Meal

Robin's parents are not rich. They have to work hard to earn a living. But they like to please their daughter when they can. She'll soon be eight years old! "That is a very special occasion!"

They decide to invite her best friends to a party and give her a big surprise. One of her father's friends, a magician, will show up right in the middle of the party!

Can you imagine the excitement when he arrives?

You can come? Wonderful.

Sharing our thoughts

1. What other things do we celebrate besides birthdays?

2. Which anniversaries mean the most to your family?

3. Can you name one or two anniversaries that are important in your country?

_____

_____

There are special anniversaries that mean a lot to every family. This is also true for the family of the children of God. In the life of the Church, there are many events we like to remember.

One of these events is so important that we want to remember it always. Read carefully the story on the next page.

An unforgettable day!

One morning, Jesus' friends were gathered in a house in Jerusalem. Peter, Andrew, and the others were very sad because a great disaster had just happened: their friend Jesus had been crucified

No one believed them. But Peter wanted to see for himself. He rushed off, with the others close behind. When they arrived … It was really true, just as the women had said. The tomb was empty!

Suddenly, some of Jesus' women friends arrived. Early that morning, before sunrise, they had gone to the tomb. Now they returned with some astounding news.

When they left, their heads were full of questions… Then the words of Jesus came back to them: "… on the third day, I shall rise." But they couldn't believe it.

One of the women, Mary Magdalene, stayed behind. Jesus had been very kind to her and she loved him deeply. Now, her heart was heavy and she was crying…

Suddenly, she sensed someone behind her. She turned and saw a man...

Woman, why do you cry? Who are you looking for?

Mary thought it was the gardener.

Sir, if you are the one who took him away, tell me where you laid him and I'll fetch him.

The man looked at her and said a single word... This simple word struck her like lightning: in that look, in that tone of voice, she recognized Someone... Yes, it was him! Deeply moved, she fell at his feet...

Mary!

Oh, Master!

Mary, go find your brothers and sisters and tell them what has happened. As for me, I shall return to my Father and yours.

When Mary rejoined the disciples, everything had changed: the sadness was gone, and joy, a most incredible joy, covered all their faces.

By now, many, such as Peter, John, and Cleophas, had also seen Jesus. All spoke of their marvelous encounter with the risen Lord!

So, it is true!

He rose just as he said he would!

Imagine yourself in the place of Mary Magdalene. Like her, you are sad because Jesus has been killed. Suddenly, he is there, before you, in his new life! He invites you to speak. What would you like to say to him?

In memory of the risen Lord...

A new life began for the friends of Jesus. The light of Easter had opened their eyes and their hearts.

Little by little, what Jesus had done and said throughout his life began to make sense to them...

They remembered his last meal and pictured themselves again at the table with him.

Many of his words came back to them.

You will no longer see me and you will be sad. But you will see me again, and you will be full of joy. And no one will be able to take away your happiness.

Take this, all of you, and eat it: this is my body, which will be given up for you. Take this, all of you, and drink it: this is the cup of my blood.

Imagine yourself at the table with Jesus and his friends. Fill in the outline of the child. Now, keep silence in your heart and try to see and hear Jesus. Slowly read his words again.

At the end of the meal, Jesus had said: **"Do this in memory of me."**
At the time, the disciples had wondered what he meant....

Now, they understood. They realized how important that meal was. When they shared the bread and wine in the memory of the risen Jesus, he was truly there with them. And that would be true for all those who would do the same, to the end of time.

That is why, just as Jesus asked them to, his friends began to meet to celebrate his farewell meal.

The day they chose was Sunday, because Jesus rose on that day. For the disciples, each Sunday was like the return of Easter, the anniversary of that extraordinary event.

At first, Christians met in each others' homes, around the dinner table.

Sometimes they had to hide because people who did not believe in Jesus wished to harm them.

Eventually the friends of the Lord moved to other countries.

They built churches where they could meet in Jesus' memory.

Some of these churches are quite beautiful. People built them to express their faith and their love for the Lord.

Easter, at our place, every Sunday!

Today, in your parish or Christian community, people gather just like Christians have done throughout the centuries.

They answer Jesus' call just as his first followers did.

1. **Do you know your parish or Christian community?**

   • It is called: _____

   • It is located at: _____

   (City, town, or neighbourhood)

2. **Who looks after your parish or Christian community?**

   • The priest: _____

   • One or two people who work with him: _____

   _____

3. **Do you know any others who belong to your parish or Christian community?**

   Name a few _____

   _____

You have just seen how important an event the Lord's meal is for us Christians. You will soon discover how this celebration is carried out.

We are invited to the Lord's Meal

To help you remember

- Easter is the greatest Christian celebration. It celebrates the day when Jesus rose from the dead.
- During his last meal, Jesus said: **"Do this in memory of me."**
- After the Resurrection, the friends of Jesus began to meet on Sundays to celebrate his last meal.
- Today, at Mass, when we share the bread and wine, we are in communion with the risen Jesus and with each other.

To follow Jesus more closely

- Over the next few weeks, try spreading joy and friendship in your family, especially at mealtimes. This would be a wonderful way to prepare yourself for sharing the Bread of Life.
- Remember to be faithful to your daily prayer.

To help you pray

You might invite your family to say a prayer before meals when you are all eating together. Here's a good one:

**Lord Jesus, bless this meal,
which we are about to share, and teach us
to be aware of the needs of others.
Amen.**

You might also, at night, ask Mary to help you prepare your heart for communion with Jesus. You can make up a prayer, or you can say the **Hail Mary.**

2 We begin the celebration

Going to Mass is not like going to the theatre to watch a play. We go to Mass to *do* something, to join in a celebration.

We listen, answer, sing, make gestures. And, of course, we watch what the priest does as he presides over the assembly. But it is all of us together who celebrate the Eucharist.

On this page is a chart telling you everything we do at Mass. By returning to it as you read this book, you'll understand better how the celebration unfolds.

	The gathering • The priest greets us. • We prepare our hearts by praying and singing.	
	The Liturgy of the Word • We listen to the Word of God. • We express our faith. • We pray for the whole world.	
	The Liturgy of the Eucharist • We give thanks to God. • We remember and celebrate Jesus' great love. • We share in the Bread of Life.	
	The farewell • The priest blesses us. • He invites us to spread the Good News.	

When you go to Mass on Sunday, sit in the first rows so you can join in fully. Remember what Jesus said: **"Let the children come to me."**

Mass is a celebration meal

These are the things we prepare:

- The altar is the table for the meal. We decorate it with candles and flowers.
- The missal is where the priest finds the prayers he needs.
- The lectionary is the big book containing the readings of the Word of God for every Sunday.
- The paten and the ciborium are the receptacles that contain the hosts.
- The chalice is the beautiful cup that contains the wine.

The priest wears special garments:

- the white alb reminds us of our Baptism.
- the coloured stole is the sign of his role as president of the assembly.
- the chasuble is a garment of celebration. Its colours change to suit the time of year.

Come celebrate the Lord's meal with joy!

Because we are all children of God and followers of Jesus, we ought to greet each other in friendship even if we don't always think of doing it.

We often sing to express our joy at being gathered in the house of God. Singing prepares our hearts to meet the Lord.

Draw the people singing. Be sure to include yourself in the group.

The priest welcomes us all in the name of the Lord by saying:

**May the grace of our Lord Jesus,
the love of God the Father,
and the fellowship of the Holy Spirit
be with you always.**

We answer:

And also with you.

**Praise God with shouts of joy,
all people!
Sing to the glory
of God's name!**

When we celebrate the Eucharist,
we are in communion with
all the Christian communities
around the world.
That is part of being Church.

But we are also in communion
with all the people of our planet,
for they are part of the human family.
God loves all people on Earth,
and all are invited to share
in God's eternal joy.

Write down the names of people you know who belong
to another Christian community or to another religion.
This will help you remember to pray for them
when you go to Mass:

_____

_____

_____

13

Preparing our hearts

There is a lovely story about a Little Prince who once met a fox in the desert.

The fox explained to the Little Prince that before you meet a friend you must "dress up your heart." That is what we do at Mass before meeting the Lord.

You already know that sin prevents us from being in communion with God and others. That is why, from the very beginning of Mass, we remember the loving tenderness of God, who always forgives us. We ask God to forgive our sins and help us walk along his paths.

The priest invites us to reflect upon our lives:

"Brothers and sisters, as we begin this Eucharist, let us all remember that we are sinners."

The congregation remains silent for a few moments. This is the time to look deep into your heart to see when you have not been loving and to tell the Lord you are sorry.

After this moment of reflection, we ask for forgiveness together, by saying or singing, for example:

Lord, have mercy.
Christ, have mercy.
Lord, have mercy.

We sing praises to God

Just like the angels at the birth of Jesus, we proclaim the great love of God by singing **Glory to God** (or a similar praise).

**Glory to God in the highest,
and peace to his people on Earth.**

**Lord God, heavenly King,
almighty God and Father,
we worship you, we give you thanks,
we praise you for your glory.**

**Lord Jesus Christ, only Son of the Father,
Lord God, Lamb of God,
you take away the sins of the world:
have mercy on us;
you are seated at the right hand of the Father:
receive our prayer.**

**For you alone are the Holy One,
you alone are the Lord,
you alone are the Most High,
Jesus Christ,
with the Holy Spirit,
in the glory of God the Father.
Amen.**

Frame this prayer with joyful colours.

After the **Glory to God,** the priest recites the **opening prayer.** He asks God that we may benefit from the celebration. At the end, we answer **"Amen,"** which means "Yes."

This is the end of the first part of the Mass: **the gathering**.
Go back to page 10 to see how it fits in with the other parts of the Mass.

To follow Jesus more closely

To help you walk along the paths of God, pray faithfully to the Lord each day, especially at morning and at night.

- You might choose a few lines from the **Glory to God,** write them on coloured paper, put them in your prayer-corner and say them as a morning prayer.

- You might say the **Our Father,** in communion with all God's children

- (You might enjoy reading over pages 20 and 21 in your Reconciliation book to enrich your prayer.)

3 We share the Word of God

At Mass, we read from the Bible. This book is very precious to us because it tells us the story of God's love for all the people of the Earth. When we read or hear stories from the Bible, we are a bit like Caroline and Paul, who learned from their grandparents their own family's story.

Caroline and Paul don't know their Grandpa and Grandma Martin very well because they live far away. But tonight Caroline and Paul are present at their grandparents' fiftieth wedding anniversary. They are so excited!

After the dinner, Grandpa and Grandma start to tell their story. They tell about their arrival here and their life out west, long, long ago.

The crossing was dangerous...

Life was hard, but we helped each other and we were happy.

Sharing our thoughts

1. Do you think that Caroline and Paul can be proud of their family story? Why?
2. Is the story of the Martin family finished or does it go on? Who will carry it on?
3. Do you know your family story? Ask someone in your family to tell you.
4. Who carries on your family story now? Write down their names. Don't forget your own!

_____   _____

_____   _____

Draw a cartoon strip of your family story and hang it in your room. Invite someone in your family to work with you.

The greatest story in the world

We Christians also have a marvelous family story to hear and tell about.

In the beginning, there was God, Father, Son, and Spirit, united in love and joy.

To share that love and joy, God created the universe and everything in it.

Planet Earth was like a beautiful, giant garden.

God wanted everyone to live there as one big family, caring for the planet and sharing its riches. This was God's beautiful Dream!

Unfortunately, people on Earth forgot about God's Dream, and soon they were fighting all the time.

Abraham, go forth... leave your country and I will make you the father of a great people.

Abraham put his trust in God. He left his home and moved to another country. When he was old, he had the great joy of having a son he called **Isaac.**

But God's great love remained faithful. So God called upon **Abraham** and made him a promise.

Abraham followed the paths of God. He spoke to God as to a friend. He taught Isaac to do the same.

Later, all the descendants of Isaac came to Egypt and prospered.

But after many years, the people of that land began to persecute them and to treat them like slaves.

God did not forget his people, and called upon **Moses** to free them.

Moses obeyed God. He led the chosen people out of Egypt, across the Red Sea, over the desert to the Promised Land.

It was in the desert that Moses gave the people of Israel the Law of God.

"You shall love the Lord your God with your whole heart. You shall love your neighbour as yourself."

Sing with joy to the Lord!

In Palestine, the Jews founded a kingdom whose leader was King **David.** Like Abraham and Moses, David taught his people to love God and to follow God's ways.

To tell God of his faith and love, David wrote beautiful prayers that we call the **psalms.** We say them to this day at Mass.

Yet people often forgot the Lord and the Law of Love. So, over the centuries, God sent messengers, **prophets,** to help them find again the way to real happiness. It was through the prophets that God made this important announcement:

One day, Someone will come.
He will be the Messiah,
the Messenger of God.
He will be the guide and saviour of all.

Prepare your hearts,
God will come to save you.

And so, at the end, came the last of the prophets: **John the Baptist...**

After his resurrection, Jesus appeared several times to his friends. They were amazed and filled with joy. Before returning to his Father, Jesus asked his followers to continue his mission, and made them a promise:

You will soon receive the Holy Spirit...

On the day of Pentecost, Jesus' friends were praying together with his mother, Mary. Suddenly, a great gust of wind filled the house. Flashes of fire touched each one of them.

They were all filled with the Holy Spirit.

Filled with courage, the disciples, led by **Peter,** left to spread around the world the Good News of the Kingdom of God.

A few years later, a Jew named Saul met the risen Jesus on the road to Damascus. From that day on, Saul, who had been the enemy of all Christians, gave himself fully to Jesus. He took the name of **Paul.** He made several difficult journeys to tell about the risen Lord.

The Lord be with you, Paul!

And the Spirit with you.

And the story continues...

The Great Story of God's Love is not yet over. Who will carry it on? Jesus, of course, who is risen and living forever. But Jesus will not do it alone. He asks us all to take part with him. That is why he gives us his Spirit. Write one thing we can do to carry on the Great Story of the Love of God.

The liturgy of the Word reminds us of our Great Story

In the first readings, we listen to the messages of the prophets and apostles. They tell us about God and teach us to do God's will.

At the end, the reader says:

This is the word of the Lord.

Everyone answers:

Glory to you, Lord

Then, as we say or sing one of King David's psalms we think about the Great Story of God's Love.

The next reading is from the Gospel. But before hearing it, we express our joy by singing or saying the **Alleluia.** This word means "Bravo! Praise the Lord!"

Gospel means Good News. There are four Gospels. They are named after disciples of Jesus: Matthew, Mark, Luke, and John.

They were written by the first Christian communities who had gathered together their recollections of Jesus.

I remember when Jesus healed the little girl...

Blessed are those who listen to God's Word and keep it in their hearts!

Out of respect for Jesus, we stand to hear the Gospel. This is what the priest says and how we answer:

The Lord be with you
– And also with you.

The Gospel of Jesus Christ according to Saint...
– Glory to you, Lord.

We make the sign of the cross on our forehead, our lips, and our heart. It is a way of saying to the Lord:

"I love your Word, I want to keep it in my spirit and in my heart. I want to share it with others."

At the end of the Gospel, the priest says:

This is the Gospel of the Lord.

We answer:

Praise to you, Lord Jesus Christ.

Then, the priest speaks to us to help us better understand the Word of God. This is called the **homily**. Sometimes, we take part in the homily by sharing what the Holy Spirit brings us to understand in the readings.

Sharing our thoughts

- What does "Alleluia" mean?
- Why do we stand at the beginning of the Gospel?
- What does "Gospel" mean?
- What gestures do we make with our hand? What do these gestures mean?

"Your word is my joy, the light of my heart." (Jeremiah 15:16)

We say that the Word of God is our joy and our light because it shows us the way of justice, friendship, and happiness. It helps us continue the Great Story of Love.

You already know the words of God quite well. There are many of them in your books.

1. Write in the sun one of God's sayings.
2. Ask someone you love to write one as well.
3. Then, together, try to answer this question: **"How does the saying I have chosen guide me, how does it bring light to my life?"**
4. You can make a little notebook with your favourite words of God. But first look at page 27.

We profess our faith

Once a year at Easter, we light a candle from the flame of the paschal candle. By doing this, we proclaim our faith in God's risen Son, Jesus, who gives us new life through Baptism.

Every Sunday, after the Gospel, we proclaim our faith again by reciting the **Creed:**

I believe in God, the Father almighty, creator of heaven and earth... I believe in Jesus Christ, his only Son, our Lord... I believe in the Holy Spirit, the holy catholic Church...

We call upon God on behalf of the whole world

The Word of God reminds us that we are all part of the same family.

Together, we must work for a better world. But it's hard. That is why we pray for one another and for the entire human family. This is what we call the **prayer of the faithful.**

During this prayer, we think of what is happening throughout the world and in our own country. We pray for all those who are hungry, sick, caught in wars and injustices.

We ask for the light and the strength to help each other, for God has made us all responsible for one another.

Someone reads our petitions and we answer:

Lord, hear our prayer.

or

Lord, answer our prayers.

Do you know what the word "petition" means? Ask someone in your family to explain it.
Write down the petitions you would like to make during Mass at your First Communion.

I will pray for _____

for _____

This is the end of the second part of the Mass: the **Liturgy of the Word.**
Go back to page 10 to see how it fits in with the other parts of the Mass.

We share the Word of God

To help you remember

- At Mass, we share the Word of God in the Bible.
- The Bible tells us the Great Story of God's Love for all the people on Earth.
- This story began when God created the universe.
- The coming of Jesus, his death, and his resurrection are the most important events in this story.
- With the Spirit of Jesus we continue to live the Great Story together by loving God and others.

To help you pray and follow Jesus more closely

The Word of God is a source of joy and hope for us, for it tells us of God's great love. It is also our light, for it shows us the paths of God.

Here's a good way to keep God's Word close by: make a small book of the Word that is all yours.

Take a few large sheets of paper. Fold them in half and make a small notebook. Add a light cardboard cover. Then tie the whole thing together with a coloured ribbon.

Look back at *We Discover God's Paths*. Read all the Words of God in it. Choose the ones you like best and write them down in your notebook. As you read through this book, do the same thing. If you have a catechism book, you can find still more. Decorate each page with drawings.

Keep your notebook in your prayer-corner. Then, any time you want to, you will be able to read God's Word. You might want to read one at night before going to sleep. This will help you feel closer to God.

4 We give thanks to the Father with Jesus

Laura and Jim's grandmother bakes her own bread. She knows that Laura and Jim love to eat it when it's warm...

Praise be to God for bread!

While they were snacking, Grandma told them the story of bread. They could see how much work it takes.

Write what the people in the pictures are doing.

_____

_____

_____

At Mass, we bring bread and wine.

Jesus chose bread and wine to give himself to us at Communion because bread and wine are the sources of life and joy.

Bread satisfies our hunger. Wine enlivens our heart. Bread and wine unite us around one table, when we share them in friendship.

Here you are with a friend bringing the bread and the wine. Complete the picture.

We praise God
for the bread and the wine

**Carefully read the two prayers the priest says
when he offers the bread and the wine to God.**

Blessed are you, Lord, God of all creation.
Through your goodness we have this bread
to offer, which earth has given and human hands
have made. It will become for us the bread of life.

- Blessed be God forever!

Blessed are you, God of all creation.
Through your goodness we have this wine
to offer, fruit of the vine and work
of human hands. It will become
our spiritual drink.

- Blessed be God forever!

- **Why do we say that it is God who gives us bread and wine?**
- **Why do we say they are the work of our hands?**

At this point in the Mass, there is usually the
collection. The money is used to maintain the
church and to help the community.

In some parishes, donations are made for the
poor, refugees, and victims of disasters.
That was also done by the first Christian
communities. They knew that disciples of
Jesus had to share what they had with those
most in need.

We are asked to give thanks

The priest asks us to pray with him:

The Lord be with you.
- And also with you.

Lift up your hearts.
- We lift them up to the Lord.

Let us give thanks to the Lord our God
- It is right to give God thanks and praise.

Do you know what it means to "give thanks"? It means "praising God with love to show our gratitude." The word "eucharist" means "thanksgiving" in Greek.

"Thank you" are among the first words you learned when you were a baby!

The words "thank you" give much happiness when they are said with love. And it hurts when they are forgotten! (Remember the ten lepers who were healed by Jesus.)

Can you remember times when you felt that happiness and that pain?

Thank you.

The Thank You game

Ask yourself whether you always remember to say thank you. To help you remember, try playing the Thank You game with your family or friends.

For three days, all players should try to notice and count the number of times in a day when there was a reason to say thank you, and they tried to do so kindly. At night, talk about it. That will show how much we need one another.

Thank you.

We give thanks to God for life

God, our Father gives us life, the beautiful universe, friendship, and joy to share with one another.

This is why, at Mass, we say a beautiful prayer of thanks that we call the **Prayer of the Eucharist.** There are many different ones. Read the one on this page. Notice how the expression "Blessed are you" appears over and over again. It means "be praised, receive thanks."

While saying the Prayer of the Eucharist, the priest opens his arms wide. What do you think this means? You might pray like that in your prayer-corner, if you wish.

God our Father, you have gathered us...

God our Father, you have brought us here together
so that we can give you thanks and praise
for all the wonderful things you have done.

We thank you for all that is beautiful in the world
and for the happiness you have given us.
We praise you for daylight
and for your word, which lights up our minds.
We praise you for the earth,
and all the people who live on it,
and for our life, which comes from you.

We know that you are good.
You love us and do great things for us.
So we all sing together:

Holy, Holy, Holy Lord, God of power and might.
Heaven and Earth are full of your glory.
Hosanna in the highest!

We Share in the Eucharist
Preparation for First Communion

On Our Way with Jesus
A Journey of Christian Initiation

Dear Parents,

The time has come to resume our journey together(*). We are about to set out on the second part of the journey toward the Lord's Table that you and your child began in *We Discover God's Paths*. We hope that the first part was a journey of spiritual intimacy and shared joy for both of you.

As before, regular family conversations and participation in the general meetings of your parish community are essential for the success of your journey.

Very affectionately, we wish you a happy journey.

Françoise
John Paul

(*) If you have not used the first book, *We Discover God's Paths*, we invite you to read pages 14 to 16 first. They will help you to use this guide more effectively.

Foreword

We Share in the Eucharist can be fully understood only when it is seen as a continuation of *We Discover God's Paths*. In that first book we were trying to awaken in each child a taste for a personal spiritual life, for a relationship with God. We also tried to prepare each child for a more conscious moral life, inspired by the life of Jesus. Finally, we hoped to give every child an opportunity to discover that trying to live in communion with God and others can truly be a path to life, joy, love, and peace.

In *We Share in the Eucharist*, we want to go one step further and help the child understand that we do not take this journey alone. Our Christian community accompanies us along the way and offers us support, especially in the sacrament of the Eucharist.

Let's be realistic

For many children Mass is "long and boring." Many would agree with the little boy who told his grandfather: "Grandpa, I don't want to go to Mass. You know I love Jesus but I hate Mass!"

When children don't like Mass, it's partly because they feel they are observing a spectacle they don't understand and are not involved in. Our goal is to help them grasp what is happening and understand that they are invited to take part in the actions that are unfolding, and that this participation can greatly enrich their communion with God and others.

What are we seeking to achieve?

We are pursuing three main goals:

- **to help children follow the unfolding of the celebration of Mass and understand the meaning of the symbols, gestures, and words that are part of it**

- **to help children see how the gestures and words in the Liturgy are connected to everyday life**

- **to help children appreciate the spiritual enrichment they can gain by taking an active part in the Mass, and to awaken in them the desire to participate**

How to get started

The parish "send-off" meeting will reawaken your child's eagerness to prepare for and receive First Communion. You should then decide together which days and times might be set aside for your conversations — and you should then start your journey right away.

A special dinner or a brief family ritual (perhaps with a card signed by everyone) could be used to wish your child "God speed" on this journey.

It is important that you help your child resume prayer habits if they have been forgotten. In *We Discover God's Paths* mini-posters were offered as a way of prompting regular prayer. In *We Share in the Eucharist*, we will instead propose a few simple suggestions at the end of each theme. At this stage it is desirable for children to develop their own prayer initiatives. But they will still need your encouragement and support.

The moral education begun in *We Discover God's Paths* must now be deepened in *We Share in the Eucharist*. Intimate conversation, based on everyday events, is very important and highly formative for your child. Because children's social and personal worlds expand beyond the family at this age, a child's conscience starts to develop quite rapidly.

When you are planning a schedule, keep in mind that the first two themes are shorter than the others. Then you won't have to rush at the end.

Theme
1 We are invited to the Lord's Meal

What are our goals?

We wish to:

- **help your child discover the meaning of the Lord's Day for the Christian community**

- **awaken in your child's heart the joy of being invited to share in the Lord's Meal**

Preparations

- **You could begin by "refreshing" your child's prayer-corner. Discuss together what you could do. For example, you might work together on a picture of the Last Supper of Jesus and write on it: "Do this in memory of me." This drawing, displayed in the prayer-corner, would stand as a symbol of this part of the journey.**

- **To help create a prayerful mood, as you did during *We Discover God's Paths*, have a candle ready that you can light during your conversations.**

Family conversations

Pages 3, 4 and 5.

- Read page 3 together. Help your child understand why feasts are important in our lives (they gather us together, unite us, give joy, etc.).

- Read pages 4 and 5 together slowly so that you can both appreciate the wonder of this marvelous Gospel story. Be sure that you both share what you would like to say to the Risen Jesus.

Pages 6, 7 and 8.

- Read the top of page 6. Then talk about the mood at the Last Supper (Jesus senses that some want him to die, he is sad and thoughtful). Read Jesus' words: *"You will not see me again…"* Point out that the disciples did not understand what Jesus meant at that moment. Ask the child what those words mean to us now, and why nobody can take away our joy.

- After you have read pages 6 and 7, point out how important it is to remember that by recreating Jesus' Last Supper, as he asked (*"Do this in memory of me"*), we truly encounter the Risen Lord.

- Work together to complete page 8. Help your child see the link between Easter and the existence of your parish or Christian community.

- Go over page 9 together. Remind your child of the importance of morning and evening prayers. Consider together how to refresh the prayer-corner

Suggestions for daily life

If the children were invited at the parish meeting to plan a share-project for Lent, you should consider following up on this idea. If they were not, it would be a good idea to come up with a family project to help prepare for sharing the Bread of Life.

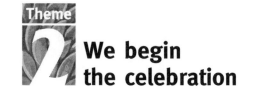

2 We begin the celebration

What are our goals?

We wish to:

- **give your child a first glimpse of the celebration: its unfolding and the objects that are used**

- **bring out the spiritual attitudes required to join the celebration fully**

- **awaken in your child the desire to prepare well for meeting the Lord in the celebration**

Preparations

Try to obtain a copy of *The Little Prince* by Antoine de Saint-Exupéry, and read together at the beginning of the week the story of the fox.

Family conversations

Pages 10, 11, 12 and 13.

- Read together, talk about and complete pages 10 and 11 so that you are sure your child understands the information on them. Then read page 12 together and invite your child to do the drawing.

- Learn by heart the prayer at the bottom of page 12. You could take turns saying it as a prayer to start your next few conversations.

Explain that the word "grace" refers to the loving benevolence of God, and God's loving presence in us. In fact, the three words: "grace," "love," and "communion" mean almost the same thing.

As you read page 13 together, talk about the people around you who follow another faith. Write down their names and religious affiliation and emphasize how we should respect other faiths.

Pages 14 and 15.

- Read page 14 together. Look back in *We Discover God's Paths* to find one of the stories that show the tremendous kindness Jesus shows towards sinners (Peter, page 31; Zaccheus, page 52; the sinful woman, page 45). Emphasize the importance of reconciliation before a celebration, and invite your child to tell a story about it.

- Page 15 ends Theme Two. *The Glory to God* is usually recited or sung, except during Advent and Lent. You might want to point out that the first two lines come from the Gospel of Saint Luke. Explain that Jesus is called the *Lamb of God* because he let himself be led to his death like a lamb, offering no resistance.

Don't forget to turn to page 10 so that your child can see how the first part of the Mass fits together with the other parts. Finally, you can invite your child to decorate the *Glory to God*.

The last part of page 15 refers briefly to prayer. This is a good opportunity to talk about morning and evening prayers, and find out if your child is experiencing any difficulty in remembering to pray regularly or needs some encouragement.

Suggestions for daily life

You might discuss with all the other members of the family the importance of trying to be at peace with one another, if necessary, before sitting down together at the family table.

Theme 3
We share the Word of God

What are our goals?

We wish to:

- **help your child discover the Bible as the Great Story of God's love, a story that we continue to live together**

- **help your child better understand how the Word of God can enlighten our lives**

- **awaken in your child's heart love of the Word and the desire to be guided by it**

Preparations

- **Have your own family photo albums available for sharing.**

- **Have a Bible nearby so that you can refer to it easily.**

- **Prepare ahead of time a few large sheets of paper, some cardboard, and coloured ribbon so that you and your child can create a Word of God notebook (see pages 25 and 27).**

- **You can enrich this theme by:**

- **organizing a get-together with grandparents or other people in the neighborhood or the town who know your family,**

- **helping your child create a comic-strip on your family story, or a family tree.**

Family conversations

Pages 16, 17, 18, 19 and 20

- Read together and talk about pages 16 and 17. Then share with your child your own family history. Talk especially about those episodes that tell of the values your family holds strongly. It would be good if many family members could take part in the activities in this theme. (If your child shares time with two parents who don't live together, it would be very good if both households become involved in sharing the child's family story. If you would like your catechist to help with any arrangements, just ask for assistance.) All the activities in this theme are about family stories. Simply choose the one that suits your family best.

- Pages 18 to 20 show that our whole Christian family also has a long history behind it, one made up of joys and sorrows, good and bad, but always filled with great hope, based on the steadfast love of God.

Pages 21, 22, 23 and 24.

- Read together and talk about pages 21 and 22. Discuss with your child how both of you can carry on the Great Story of God's love by walking along God's paths.

- Read page 23 together, then show the Gospels to your child. Point out again the names of the four evangelists. Finally, together find a story in the Gospels that your child knows and likes.

- On page 24, draw your child's attention to the practice of making the sign of the cross. Do it together and suggest that together you learn by heart the short prayer on the page: *"I love your Word, I want to keep it in my mind and in my heart. I want to share it with others."* You could make the sign of the cross and say this prayer together before reading one of the Gospel stories. This is also a good opportunity to have your child memorize the two kinds of responses that follow the readings: *Glory be to God* and *Praise to you, Lord Jesus.*

Pages 25, 26 and 27

- The first part of page 25 continues an activity about the Word of God. Take all the time you need for the first three parts of the activity. Show your child how the Word of God guides our adult lives. For example, you could talk about how God's Word helps us make decisions and learn to forgive others, and gives us hope and courage at the time of the death of a loved one.

Encourage your child to prepare a booklet on the Word of God. You could start it together over the next few days. Your child could choose the words and make the drawings and you might help write the words, if necessary.

- This page ends with the mention of the word "Creed." Tell your child that this word comes from the Latin "Credo," which means *I believe.* Point out how amazing and wonderful it is that people have shared our faith over many centuries and still do so today all around the world.

- After the Creed comes the Prayer of the Faithful. Be sure to think of petitions that are meaningful to you both. You can also use current news stories to help. Finally, remember to return to page 10 to show your child how this part of the Mass fits with the other parts.

While your child is preparing the booklet on the Word of God, emphasize the tremendous value of the Word of God in guiding us on God's paths.

Suggestions for daily life

In the weeks to come, encourage your child to add to the booklet on the Word of God and to use it for morning and evening prayers. For morning prayer, short quotes might be written on strips of paper and put in the prayer-corner. When waking up, your child can, at a glance, be reminded of God's presence.

Enrichment activities

- Plan a meeting with older family members, like grandparents, aunts and uncles, and ask them to tell your child some of their family recollections. If they live far away, your child could ask them to send a letter about some of their fondest memories.

- Create a family tree.

- Design a cartoon strip about your family's history.
- Draw up a chart showing your family's most important values.
- Develop together a family motto.

Note: If the parish offers children an opportunity to celebrate the Sacrament of Reconciliation during Lent, you could help the child prepare, as you did the first time, with the help of *We Discover God's Paths*.

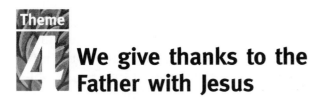

4 We give thanks to the Father with Jesus

What are our goals?

We wish to:

- **help your child discover that thanksgiving is at the heart of the Eucharist just as it is at the heart of our Christian lives**

- **help your child understand the symbolic meaning of sharing bread and wine**

- **reaffirm your child's desire to give thanks to God and to show gratitude to others**

Preparations

Prepare ahead of time what you need to create a large family poster or a mobile (paper, glue, string, coloured pencils); also gather the ingredients for baking a very special loaf of bread.

Family conversations

Pages 28, 29 and 30

- Read together the story of Laura and Jim on pages 28 and 29 and talk together about times when you've eaten delicious bread. Then, help your child see the link between this story and sharing the bread and wine at Mass. Work together on the two activities on page 29.

This section provides a good opportunity to talk again about the mood at family meals. You could go back to page 36 in *We Discover God's Paths* to see how to improve the feeling around the family table so that everyone finds joy and encouragement there.

- Read together the prayers on page 30 and then invite your child to respond to the two questions.

When you read about the collection, make the connection between that part of the Mass and the share project, which was proposed at the parish "send-off" meeting.

Pages 31, 32 and 33.

- Page 31 marks the beginning of the **Liturgy of the Eucharist**. Make sure your child understands the meaning of the word. Ask your child to tell the story of the ten lepers healed by Jesus, or reread together page 42 in *We Discover God's Paths*. Search together for overlooked opportunities to say "thank you." Then decide when and where you will play the *Thank You* game.

- Before reading page 32, ask your child to show, through gestures and without speaking, different ways of expressing joy when presented with a magnificent gift. (You should do it as well.) Then draw your child's attention to the priest's wide-arm gesture on page 31 and point out the connection between his body language and the Prayer of the Eucharist. Read the prayer together.

On page 33 share some memories for which you would like to give thanks. Then complete the album together.

You can now say together the Prayer of the Eucharist (page 32) or suggest it be said for the evening prayer.

End this conversation with the questions at the bottom of page 33. Share your own experiences, too.

Pages 34, 35, 36 and 37.

- Look at the picture of Jesus on page 34, and share your feelings about Jesus. Reread together pages 21 and 22 and then ask your child to complete the activity at the bottom of the page.

- Read page 35 together. After the child does the drawing, mention the story of Jesus that you like most and explain why.

Don't forget to turn to page 10 to see how this part fits with the other parts of the Mass.

- Page 36 presents a simple prayer through which your child can feel united with Christians throughout the world. Encourage him or her to learn this prayer and the gestures by heart. To help develop the prayer habit, offer to join in saying it for the next several mornings.

- Make sure your child understands the four key points at the top of page 37.

Suggestions for daily life

- As suggested in "To follow Jesus more closely" and "To help you pray" on page 37,

try to encourage your child to persevere in the habit of expressing thanks to God as well as to those close to him or her.

- You could also play the *Breath of Life* game together (see *We Discover God's Paths*, page 10). The game is a good introduction to a thanksgiving prayer for the gift of life.

Enrichment activities

- Offer to work with your child to prepare a loaf of home-made bread. Then you can invite some friends to share it. Or, you might instead share it at a family meal and present it with a short poem about the joy of coming together around the family table to share our own bread of life.

- Create a Thanksgiving poster (or a mobile) with the whole family. Invite each family member to recall something for which they would like to give thanks. Use photos, drawings, magazine clippings, short texts, etc., to illustrate the poster. Help your child arrange all the parts together and then write a prayer of praise to go on the poster. Then it can be hung prominently at home or in the prayer-corner.

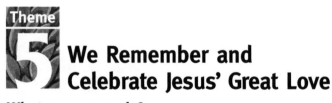

Theme

5 We Remember and Celebrate Jesus' Great Love

What are our goals?

We wish to:

- **help your child grasp, in a way he or she can understand, that the Paschal mystery is at the heart of our faith and our Eucharist celebration**

- **strengthen in your child's heart the joy of Christian hope**

- **help your child begin to understand what is meant by "giving our life like Jesus" and encourage this giving in everyday life**

Family conversations

Pages 38, 39 and 40.

• When you read together about remembering and celebrating important events in our lives, remind the child that, at Mass, we do far more than remember Jesus. We actually meet the Risen Lord.

If you have a copy of the Gospels, you could read ahead of time the complete text of Jesus washing his disciples' feet (John 13:1-17), and then re-tell it to your child. Or you could read the Gospel account together on page 38. Emphasize the startling aspect of what Jesus did. Then talk about the opportunities we have for placing ourselves at the service of others.

• Page 39 is one of the most important in the theme. Take time to go over it slowly, and make sure your child sees the connection between the Last Supper and the Mass. Then help your child complete the activity at the bottom of the page.

• Page 40. Look at the drawing together. Then discuss the four questions to ensure that your child understands the symbolism of the cross: the cross reminds us of the death of Jesus, and the light speaks to us of the resurrection. The cross is a sign of hope. It reminds us that Jesus saves us from sin and death and promises us resurrection.

Invite your child to learn the two acclamations and use them in turn as an evening prayer during the two weeks leading up to Easter.

Pages 41, 42 and 43.

• Read together the story of Sam and Alex on pages 41 and 42. Use the four questions on page 42 to help you emphasize that loving means being ready, from time to time, to make sacrifices for those we love.

Give your child all the time needed to complete the two activities at the bottom of page 42. Share one of your own experiences.

Emphasize the special joy we find when we are able to love as Jesus did. It is God's own joy!

• The central idea on page 43 is that of being in "communion in prayer with the whole Church." Saint Paul uses the image of a body to illustrate this connection among all Christians. Our limbs may be different but they are all equally important and share in the same life. The body of the Church is the same. We are accepted with all our differences and joined into one single body, the body of the Risen Christ. When you read this page, remind your child about the different people who make up the Church (including those who have died) and for whom we pray during the Eucharist.

Pages 44, 45, 46 and 47.

• Before reading page 44, ask your child to remember an especially enjoyable party and to think about this question: "Why was everyone at the party so happy?" (We were together, we were joined in friendship, we were having a good time, etc.)

Then ask how it felt after the party. (We're sorry that it was over so soon. We wanted it to go on longer…) Then tell your child that although we know very little about life everlasting, writers in the Bible compare it to a wonderful feast that will last forever.

Some children may be curious about heaven and death, or even frightened. Be open to any questions or feelings your child may have, and don't feel you must try to explain what we cannot understand. The Word of God does not offer us an explanation but rather *hope*: Because of the great love of God and the resurrection of Jesus, we trust in Jesus' promise.

• Together look at the drawing on pages 44 and 45 and ask your child to talk about it. Read together the words at the top of page 46. Before reading St. John's poem, take a moment of silence. Ask the Holy Spirit to open your hearts to the joy of hope. Then, slowly read aloud the beautiful text: *I saw a new heaven…*

- Page 46 represents the culmination of the theme. We come to the conclusion of the great Prayer of the Eucharist where, together with Jesus, we offer ourselves to the Father.

Together, look carefully at the pictures. Help your child understand the following ideas:

- Through the bread and wine, Jesus himself is the one offered by the priest and the Christian congregation to God

- We are all invited to offer our life with Jesus

- Offering our lives means offering our everyday work, our joys and sorrows, and all that we do.

After your child identifies in the thought bubbles the two scenes of everyday life, ask your child to say what he or she would like to offer especially to Jesus, and then to draw it in the empty bubble. Finally, learn by heart together the ending of the Prayer of the Eucharist: *Through him, with him...* Explain that the pronoun "him" refers to the Risen Christ.

- Carefully read together the three summary statements at to the top of page 47. Make sure your child understands them. Remember to return to page 10 to see how this part fits with the other parts of the Mass.

When you read together the second section "To follow Jesus more closely," help your child name what she or he plans to do during the weeks leading up to Easter and to First Communion. Share your own ideas and plans too.

Suggestions for daily life

- Remind your child of the different suggestions for prayer in the last section on page 47. Share moments of prayer together as often as possible.

- Encourage your child to enrich the Word book by adding new texts.

- Remember to keep up with the shared project.

Footnote

Theme Five normally brings you to the beginning of Holy Week. Theme Six should start only after Easter. This pause in the journey allows you to participate more easily during the week of preparations leading up to Easter. You could, as a part of your Easter preparation, take time to tell the child a few episodes from the Passion, drawing, for instance, on Luke, chapter 22, verses 39 to 71 and chapter 23.

If you are able to take your child to any of the Holy Week celebrations, try to make sure that you both can see what goes on and can take part.

Enrichment Activities

It would be a wonderful idea to invite your child to prepare together a special ritual for the family Easter meal. Here are a few suggestions.

- Prepare together a special bread or cake in the shape of a crown. Decorate the plate with a beautiful large candle and with signs of life and joy: a cutout butterfly, the word "Alleluia," and anything else you can think of together. Gather round the table where the candle is placed and sing a brief Paschal acclamation like:

   "Christ our Light." "Thanks be to God."

Repeat the acclamation while your child lights the candle. Then ask your child to tell the story of one of Jesus' appearances to his followers. Then wish one another Happy Easter and invite your child, or perhaps another child in the family, to say grace. Now enjoy the meal!

We share the Bread of Life

What are our goals?

We wish to:

- help your child see that in the sharing of the Eucharist it is truly the Risen Jesus giving himself to us

- help your child grasp the deep meaning of the expression "living in communion with Jesus in daily life"

- affirm your child's desire to meet Jesus through the Eucharist

Family conversations

Pages 48, 49, 50 and 51

- Page 48 explores the meaning of the expression "being in communion" with someone. Talk with your child about each of the illustrated situations. Then share with your child the names of the people with whom you feel you are "in communion."

If there are people who are far away and with whom you and your child wish to get in touch again, this might be a good opportunity to discuss what gesture of "communion" would be best.

- Pages 49 and 50 deepen the explanation of what it means to be "in communion" with someone. Let your child retell you the story of Elizabeth and Mark's family. Use the three questions on page 50 to ensure that the message has been understood. (We can live "in communion" with someone even if we don't see that person, and there are many ways to help us stay "in communion.") Remind your child that the prayer-corner contains signs that help keep us in communion with God.

- Page 51 discusses how the sacraments are "signs of communion" given to us by Jesus

so that we can live in communion with God and each other. Help your child understand the meaning of the sacraments, and then write down the names of the three sacraments that are mentioned.

Pages 52, 53 and 54.

- Page 52 serves as an introduction to everything that follows. It tells the story of the miracle of the loaves of bread, which announces and prefigures the Eucharistic communion.

Read together the first part of the story. To help your child identify with the young child in the scene, ask what that child might have felt:

- when no one had any food to eat

- when Jesus asked for the bread and fish

- when Jesus miraculously shared the five loaves and two fish with the crowd of five thousand people.

Then read together and talk about the second part of the page. Encourage your child to learn by heart with you these words of Jesus, which give so much hope: *I am the Living Bread, come down from heaven …*

- Pages 53 and 54 present the last preparations and prayers before Communion.

If your child's memory of the *Our Father* is a little unsure, you can work together on it. If your child already knows the *Our Father,* you can place the emphasis on the wish for peace that is presented to us by the priest. You can ask your child if she or he might need to be reconciled with someone before First Communion day. If so, help ensure that the opportunity is created.

Page 54 recounts the story of the Roman centurion. In order to talk about this story more easily, you could first read it in Luke (Lk 7: 1-12). Use the four questions to help your child understand the text. Help your child see that we need to be healed of our shortcomings, our lack of love, our grudges. Emphasize that by coming to us in Communion, Jesus gives us his Spirit to help us grow in love. Finally, invite your child to learn with you the prayer: *"Lord, I am not worthy to receive you, but only say the word and I shall be healed."*

Pages 55, 56, 57 and 58.

- We have now arrived at Communion time. Read together the first paragraph on page 55. Tell your child about people with whom you share your joys and sorrows. Emphasize how precious these moments and these people are. Then read the Gospel scene. Point out the love that Jesus has always had for children, and remind your child that we can tell Jesus anything and share everything with him. Jesus always welcomes and understands us.

Share together the suggested meditation prayer, and invite your child to complete the two drawings.

- On page 56 point out the quiet and respectful attitude of the children receiving Communion. This might be a good opportunity to show again how the host is received.

- The illustrations on page 57 show children praying, kneeling, singing, and meditating. It's a good idea to point these out since often the excitement of the day causes children to forget the magnitude of the mystery they are living at that moment.

- Finally, read page 58 together. Review whatever you think your child does not understand well. Return to page 10 to see how the sharing of the Bread of Life fits in with the other parts of the Mass.

Invite your child to quietly re-read, that night, the last two sections: "To better follow Jesus" and "To help you pray this week."

Suggestions for daily life

- It is normal for a child to feel a great deal of excitement at the thought of the celebration being prepared at home. However, it is important not to let these preparations absorb all your child's attention. Try to show the link between this home celebration and the spiritual celebration that is about to take place. Make sure to take all the time needed for the usual conversations and for evening prayer.

- Don't forget to have all the guests sign the last page of your child's book.

7 We are sent to share the joy of God

What are our goals?

We wish to:

- help your child understand that "living in communion with Jesus" means trying to walk with him on the paths of God to build a better world together;

- affirm your child's confidence that, together with Jesus, we can walk on God's paths.

Preparations

It is important for your child to express gratitude to all the people who travelled together on this journey throughout the year: the catechist, those responsible for meetings, the parish priest, etc. Your child could, for example, send them a nice picture with a word of thanks, or perhaps a photograph of the celebration. Discuss together what your child would like to do.

- Pages 59 and 60 tell about the disciples meeting with the Risen Jesus on the road to Emmaus. This Gospel story is very important because it reflects the situation we Christians find ourselves in today. We too can truly meet the Risen Lord, but we have to recognize him in signs he has given us. It would be best to discuss this story when you have lots of time. Use the questions on page 60 to help you.

- Invite your child to find similarities between the story of the two disciples and what he or she has lived over the past year. Help your child see that various people (yourself, the catechist, the priest, etc.) have given their help for the child to understand the Word of God, to discover God's ways. These people are like signs of the presence and love of the Risen Lord. The Lord then came to give himself to the child as the Bread of Life.

- Read together and talk about page 61. Help your child realize that knowing the love of God and the great hope brought by Jesus makes us responsible for one another. This is what it means to be Christian. We are called to share the Great Dream of God; we are called to do our part in building a better world.

- Page 62, the last of the theme, continues the message of page 61. Your child is invited to see how he or she can continue the journey with Jesus. Emphasize the importance of prayer, and try together to identify efforts that could be made in everyday life. Remember to offer your help.

Finally, invite your child to take a moment of reflection before writing the prayer, so that it will truly come from the heart.

A task to be carried on

The celebration is over, but life goes on — and your child still needs you. The coming months are very important for spiritual development. Without help on your part, this First Communion may remain a lovely memory but one with no tomorrow. With your daily support, however, it can mark a significant development in your child's personal relationship with the Lord. And we know this will be the most precious life-long gift your child can receive.

If you did not use *We Discover God's Paths*, the following pages will help you to use this book.

Dear Parents,

You have asked your Christian community to welcome your child to the Lord's Table. This is an important step in a child's spiritual development. Indeed it will be the first time your child has the opportunity to freely express in public his or her faith and desire to follow Jesus. Your Christian community is eager to cooperate wholeheartedly with you so this step will be a truly meaningful and enjoyable experience for your child.

A few years ago, you asked for your child to be baptized. Maybe you did it out of a deep Christian conviction, or perhaps to follow a family tradition. Whatever the reason, the Church gladly welcomed your child and, in turn, invited you to share your faith with your child. Perhaps you responded to this invitation ... but life is so busy when you have young children, and time goes by so quickly. Perhaps time went by without letting you put your mind to the task.

One thing is certain: whether you are aware of it or not, you have been for your child, over the years, the first sign, the first sacrament of God's love. Indeed, it is only through the simple gestures of your daily loving care that your child's heart and mind has been able to open up to faith and trust in God's infinite tenderness.

Now, with the upcoming celebration of First Communion, you are invited to share in the very special experience of preparing your child — in your own home, at your own pace.

Of course, since your child's baptism, a number of things may have changed in your personal or family life. You may have lost touch with the Church for different reasons. Whatever your situation, as long as you have a genuine desire to share with your child the Christian faith and hope that helps you live your own life, your Christian community is convinced that no one is better equipped for this task of preparing your child than you. No one can do it as well simply because no one is closer to your child than you are.

Be assured, however, that your Christian community will provide support and will walk with you on this very special journey. This book is also intended to help make the journey easy and enjoyable for you and your child. It is not a school book that emphasizes teaching and lesson plans. Instead it is a simple Family Guide to help you during an intensive stage of your child's moral and spiritual formation.

We hope that the stories and pictures in your child's book will offer you an exciting starting point for one-on-one conversations with your child. And you know how much your child appreciates special time with you! In fact, surveys have shown that spending more time with their parents is the number one wish for today's children. It is our hope and conviction that the journey offered here will be, for you and your child, a wonderful experience, bringing you even closer to each other and to the Lord.

Francoise

John Paul

SOME PRACTICAL CONSIDERATIONS

What are we hoping to accomplish?

Preparing children for the Sacrament of Reconciliation involves more than getting them ready for a ceremony. It should also do the following:

- **teach children to see themselves in the light of God's love. This strengthens their self-esteem and at the same time makes it easier to accept their personal limitations and shortcomings**

- **help children discover that Jesus shows us the way to the true happiness God wants for us**

- **encourage children to develop simple habits that will sustain their spiritual life, while strengthening their character**

- **gradually enable children to acquire a more precise sense of right and wrong and to make their own moral decisions.**

- **instill in children a deep trust in the infinite love of God, who always forgives us.**

Our approach

This journey is built upon two very important foundations.

1. Regular conversations with your child

All you have to do is read a few pages together with your child and use the questions provided and your child's reactions to the stories, pictures, and questions as the starting point for conversations.

Once you've finished reading and talking, each theme offers activities: a drawing, short sentences to complete, a game to play together, and so on. When possible, it's better to complete the activity immediately following your conversation. If you can't always do that, it's important that you recapture the spirit of the shared time together before starting the activity.

When your child has finished an activity, take time to admire what your child has done. Ask your child to tell you about it. Always remember to share your own comments and reactions.

We often suggest a short prayer during or at the end of your time together.

2. Special attention to your child's daily life

This journey of preparation is an intense time of apprenticeship in Christian living. It is important to be more attentive than usual to your child's good and bad experiences, so you can discuss them and reflect on them together. This doesn't mean that you are to watch over and criticize your child. Just the opposite! A child needs encouragement just as a plant needs water. Encourage your child to put into practice what is discovered at each step on this journey and never to give up trying.

Preparing for a theme

Before starting a theme, take the time to read everything related to it both in your child's book and in this Guide. Then decide how many conversations you will need to experience the theme with your child without having to rush. The themes are organized so that there is a flow within each theme and a continuity from one theme to the next. The grouping of the pages only indicates that there is a link between them. Feel free to organize your times together as you wish.

Preparing together

A good conversation needs to be experienced in an atmosphere of joy, peace, and prayer. The following suggestions might help create such an atmosphere.

- **Discuss with your child the best time for your conversations. Stick to the agreed-upon schedule except when there is an unexpected interruption.**

- **Choose a place where you won't be disturbed and ask other family members to respect this time** you've put aside. Older children may be a bit jealous, but that's a good sign. They, too, would like to have more time with you. Younger ones can start to look forward to the time when it will be their turn!

- A candle or vigil light on the table can help create a prayerful atmosphere. Before starting, share a moment of silence together so that you can become aware of God's presence. Share a short prayer or a prayerful wish like:

"The Lord is with you."
"And also with you."
or
"The peace of Christ be with you."
"And also with you."

You are now ready for this special time for you, your child, and God.

An important habit to develop

This journey provides a good opportunity to develop the habit of daily prayer, a habit that will be of great importance for your child's life as a Christian in years to come. It is a good idea to set aside a few minutes each evening, or whenever possible, to pray with your child. Remember that this means praying with your child, and not just listening to your child's prayers. Each theme provides simple suggestions that can make this time a rich and joy-filled experience for you both. At the centre of the first book (*We Discover God's Paths*) you will find four mini posters – one for each theme. Cut them out and give one to your child at the beginning of each theme. Read the prayer together and invite your child to colour it and to put it in the prayer-corner.

Celebrate the start of the journey

Celebrate your child's "first step" with a simple gesture. You might, for example, make a special dessert for the evening meal. Give your child a nice card signed by all the family with thoughts and blessings for a "happy journey." This would be a good opportunity to discuss the time you'll be spending with your child and to ask other family members to respect that time. Your child's godparents or grandparents could be invited to the meal, too.

If you are separated or divorced, it's best, whenever possible, for both parents to be aware of your child's journey, and to be involved as much as possible throughout the year, especially if the child spends weekends or holidays at different homes. If you wish, the parish catechist can help you make suitable arrangements.

This Family Guide is an integral part of the preparation for first communion book *We Share in the Eucharist*.

Authors: Francoise D'Arcy Berube and John Paul Berube

Graphic Design: Brian Lehen Graphic • Design Ltd

Imprimatur: Most Rev. Marcel Gervais, Archbishop of Ottawa, 24 February, 1997.

© 1997 Novalis Publishing, 49 Front Street East, 2nd Floor, Toronto, Ontaro M5E 1B3, Canada. Tel: 1-800-387-7154. Fax: (416) 363-9409.

E-mail: novalis@interlog.com

ISBN: 2-89088-858-4

Distributed in Great Britain and Ireland by Geoffrey Chapman, an imprint of Cassell, Wellington House, 125 Strand, London WC2R 0BB

Think back to the happy memories for which you would like to thank the Lord. Draw them in the empty spaces of the album.

Then, with all your heart, say the beautiful prayer of praise on the previous page. The word **"Hosanna"** is a shout of joy and confidence in Hebrew.

Do you sometimes think of giving thanks to God during the day?

Do you most feel like doing it:

- **when you see something beautiful?**
- **when you experience an especially joyful moment?**
- **when you feel the joy of loving like Jesus?**

We give thanks especially for Jesus

**The greatest of the gifts of God
is Jesus, the Lord, God's own Son!**

**"God
so loved us
that He gave us
His only Son."**
(John 3:16)

**Reread the Great Story of God's Love (from pages 21 to 23).
Think of what Jesus has done and continues to do for us. Write it here:**

Jesus _____

Jesus _____

This is why I want to praise God and give thanks in the Eucharist.

Father, you are always thinking
about your people; you never forget us.
You sent your Son Jesus,
who gave his life for us
and who came to save us.

He cured sick people;
he cared for those who were poor
and wept with those who were sad.
He forgave sinners and taught us
to forgive each other.

He loved everyone
and showed us how to be kind.
He took children in his arms
and blessed them.

So we all sing together:

**Blessed is He who comes in the name of the Lord.
Hosanna in the highest!**

Draw one of your favourite stories of Jesus.

When we say:

**"Blessed is He
who comes in the name
of the Lord"**

we think of

_____

This is the end
of the first stage of the
Liturgy of the Eucharist.
Go back to page 10 to see
how it fits in with the other
parts of the Mass.

The most beautiful morning prayer

At any moment in the day, somewhere in the world the Eucharist is being celebrated. The most beautiful morning prayer you could say is to join this great thanksgiving. Here's how you can do it. It will only take a minute and you will be in communion with Christians all over the world.

- Stretch your body so that you feel good.
- Then stand straight on both feet. Close your eyes. Imagine yourself standing on our beautiful planet Earth!
- Breathe deeply two or three times. Remember that God is looking at you with love.
  Then pray this way:

Dear God, here I am.

Giving thanks for this day.

With Jesus, your Son,

I give you this day.

I give you my love

and with him I pray

your Kingdom **may come!**

We give thanks to the Father with Jesus

To help you remember

1. With bread and wine we celebrate Jesus' meal.
2. The word eucharist means "thanksgiving."
3. Giving thanks means praising God with love to express our gratitude.
4. At Mass, we give thanks for life, for the universe and for Jesus, the most beautiful of God's gifts.

To follow Jesus more closely

Here is what you could do:

- Open your eyes and heart to notice the many opportunities you have to say thank you with kindness.
- Think sometimes of all that your family and other people do for you. Try to imagine something special that you could do to show your thanks.
- Remember to give thanks to the Lord during the day.

To help you pray

- You could say the prayers of praise on pages 32 or 35.
- You could learn the Prayer of Offering on page 36 and get into the habit of saying it every morning.

5 We remember and celebrate Jesus' great love

We like to remember and celebrate the important events in our lives.
When parents celebrate your birthday, they relive the great joy of your birth.

At Mass, we celebrate Jesus by remembering his last meal, his death, and his resurrection. But there is a great deal more, of course, for during the Eucharist the risen Jesus himself comes among us.

To prepare his friends for his farewell meal, Jesus did something very surprising. He had noticed that they would often argue about who was the leader or who was the best. So, he gave them an example they would never forget.

At that time in Palestine people walked barefoot or in sandals.

The roads were very dusty. That is why, when a guest was invited to someone's home, a servant would come to wash the guest's feet in a basin of water.

That night, Jesus, the Son of the almighty God, made himself the servant of his friends.

Do you understand what I have done? You call me Master and Lord, and you do well for that is what I am. I have given you an example so you will do as I did. Put yourself at each other's service.

What do you think Jesus was trying to teach that day?

The priest continues the Prayer of the Eucharist by telling the story of the Last Supper, the last meal of Jesus. He repeats the gestures and the words of Jesus. But first he calls upon the Holy Spirit:

God, our Father, we now ask you to send your Holy Spirit to change these gifts of bread and wine into the body and the blood of Jesus Christ, our Lord.

He then takes the bread in his hands and says, as Jesus had:

Take this, all of you, and eat it: this is my body, which will be given up for you.

Then, the priest takes the cup of wine and says, as Jesus had:

Take this, all of you, and drink from it: this is the cup of my blood.

After each of these words, the priest shows us the bread, then the wine, which have become, through the Holy Spirit, the presence of the risen Jesus among us.

What is the story behind these two pictures?

• The first one tells of _____

• The second one tells of _____

Why are these two pictures on the same page?

_____

We joyfully proclaim the risen Jesus

At the Last Supper, the apostles saw Jesus with their own eyes. At Mass, we do not see him. But we are certain that he is with us. That is why the priest invites us to proclaim our faith:

Let us proclaim the mystery of faith.

We reply with a joyful acclamation, such as one of the following:

**Christ has died,
Christ has risen,
Christ will come again**

**Dying you destroyed our death,
rising you restored our life,
Lord Jesus, come in glory.**

Think of what you have just read. Look carefully at the picture and then answer these questions:

1. What does the cross remind us of?

2. What does the light that surrounds it remind us of?

3. Why is the cross planted on planet Earth?

4. Why is the cross a symbol of joy and hope for us?

In the two acclamations on this page, we recall three important events concerning Jesus. They are:

His _____

His _____

His _____

We learn to give our life as Jesus did

After giving them the bread and the wine, Jesus told his friends: "Do this in memory of me." He meant two things. First, of course, "Celebrate this meal in memory of me." That is what we do at Mass. But Jesus was also inviting us to follow him on the paths of love, even when it's hard, even when it requires sacrifices. Jesus really meant:

"In memory of me, love one another as I have loved you."

When we do something that requires a great deal of love, we make a sacrifice. And when we sacrifice for someone, we are a little like Jesus, for we learn to give our life as Jesus did. Here is how Alex tried to do it.

Sharing our thoughts

1. What was Alex's sacrifice?
2. Why did Alex do it?
3. What did Sam think when he saw Alex?
4. How did Alex feel when he saw how happy Sam was? Why?

Does anyone make sacrifices for you? Write down their names and what they do.

Can you remember a sacrifice you made for someone? Draw a picture of what you did.

- Why did you do it?
- How did it make you feel? Why?

You will be known as my followers by the love you show one another. (John 13:35)

We pray in communion with the whole Church

The Church is like a big family. We need one another and we try to help each other follow the paths of God. The apostle Paul compared the Church to a large body whose members share the same life, the life of the risen Jesus.

There are many different parts to our body. We have eyes, ears, hands, and feet… and each part needs all the others. They all share one life, as part of the same body.

In Church it is the same. So we express our joy at being united into one body by the Spirit of Jesus, as we pray for the Church throughout the whole world.

Read the following prayer and fill in the missing parts:

**Lord our God, listen to our prayer.
Send the Holy Spirit to all of us
who share in this meal.**

**May this Spirit
bring us closer together
in the family of the Church, with
our Pope _____,
our Bishop _____,
all other bishops, and all
who serve your people.**

**Don't forget those we love
and those we do not love enough.**

**Remember those who have died.
Receive them with love in your home.**

In the box, write the name and place a photo or drawing of a person you have loved and who has joined the Lord.

43

We prepare for the great heavenly feast

When we celebrate the Eucharist,
we open our hearts wide to the great Christian hope.

We remember that God created us out of love
to share eternal life and joy.

We remember that the paths of God,
sometimes hard to follow,
lead us to God's eternal Kingdom.

We remember that the risen Jesus promised
that he would return one day in glory
to take us to him and "make all things new again."

That is why we pray:

Gather us all together into your Kingdom.
There we shall be happy forever
with the Virgin Mary,
Mother of God and our mother.
There all the friends of Jesus
the Lord will sing a song of joy.

We await your return, Lord Jesus!

Heaven and eternal life are great mysteries that we can't fully understand. But they inspire our dreams. Poets speak of them as a marvelous feast that never ends. This is how Saint John helps us to imagine it:

I saw a new heaven and a new earth.
I saw a Holy City that came down from
beside God.
It shone like a precious gem.
The River of Life flows through it,
clear as crystal!

The Holy City no longer needs a sun
or a moon,
for the Glory of God illuminates it!

All the people of the world march towards it.
It is the home of God and all people.

And God will wipe away all the tears from their eyes.
There will be no more death, no more cries,
no more pain, for the old world will be gone…

And God said:
"Thus I make all things new!"

Jesus promised us:

"I will return for you and take you with me so that
where I am, there will you be."

We can answer him:

"Come, Lord Jesus, come. We will go in joy
to the City of God!"

We offer our life with Jesus

We started the Prayer of the Eucharist by offering God bread and wine. Through the Holy Spirit, they became the presence of the risen Lord among us.

And now, it is the risen Lord himself that we offer to the Father, with our praise, to end the Prayer of the Eucharist:

**Through him, with him, in him,
in the unity of the Holy Spirit,
all glory and honour is yours,
almighty Father,
for ever and ever.**

We sing or say with all our hearts: **Amen.**

Just like the people in this picture, you too can offer to God your daily work and your efforts to love the way Jesus did.

Draw your offering in the empty bubble.

We remember and celebrate Jesus' great love

To help you remember

At Mass

- we remember the last meal of Jesus, his death, and his resurrection,
- we learn to give our life as he did,
- we strengthen our hope for eternal life.

Go back to page 10 to see where this part of the Mass fits in with the other parts.

To follow Jesus more closely

Ask yourself if you have the determination to make the little sacrifices that are needed to walk, like Jesus, along the paths of love. Try to act generously over the coming weeks, to prepare your heart to receive the Lord Jesus in the Eucharist.

To help you pray

- You might read page 38 and imagine yourself in the story. Then do a meditation prayer.
- Use the acclamations on page 40 or the prayer on page 44.
- Read St. John's poem on page 45 and then offer a silent prayer with the last words of the poem:
    > *"Come, Lord Jesus, come.*
    > *We will go in joy to the City of God."*

6 We share the Bread of Life

In a few days, you will receive your First Communion! To understand exactly what the word "Communion" means, look at the following pictures and answer the questions.

Are these children **"in communion"** with one another? _____

And these? _____

And what about these people? _____

Are these people **"in communion"** with one another? _____

What about these? _____

Write the names of people with whom you are most often "in communion."

_____

Can you explain why you are "in communion" with them?

We can still be in communion with someone who's not with us...

Elizabeth and Mark's dad had to travel around the world for three months on business. Everybody felt a little sad, but they were all determined to stay in communion.

Mark set the table at night, always setting a place for their father. They often talked about him during supper.

Elizabeth bought herself a lovely plant that she placed in front of her dad's photograph in her room. She prayed for him every night.

Their mom often wrote to their dad and sent him photos.

Father left his favourite rosebush in Mark's care. He left detailed instructions for him to follow.

Father sent postcards of the places he visited. They were all hung up in the hallway. They also put up a map and a calendar so that everyone could follow his travels. That way, they always felt close to him.

Father had left a secret present for their mom's birthday. He had asked the children to give it to her along with their own.

On their mom's birthday, their dad had a beautiful bouquet delivered to her.

Sharing our thoughts

1. Does the bouquet mean the same thing to the messenger as to Mark and Elizabeth's mother?

2. Write into the bubbles what the messenger might think about the bouquet and what Mark and Elizabeth's mother is thinking as she arranges the flowers.

3. When people love each other and are apart, they can remain in communion through signs. Name all the signs (things, words, and actions) that allowed Elizabeth and Mark's family to remain in communion.

That night, he phoned from the other end of the world to wish her "Happy Birthday!"

Happy Birthday!

When people really love and understand each other, they are in communion.
When they share a dream or a project and work together to make it happen,
they are in communion.

God, our Father, the Lord Jesus, and the Holy Spirit want to be in communion with us. They give us the sacraments to help us live this communion.

We can live in communion with God

The sacraments are signs of love that Jesus has given us to allow us to live in communion with God and one another.

Fill in the names of the sacraments:

- In _____, Jesus tells you, through the sign of water:
  "God, my Father, loves you. You are God's own child."

- In _____, Jesus tells you through the gesture of the priest:
  "Your sins are forgiven. Go in peace."

- In _____, Jesus tells you through the sign of the shared bread:
  "I am the living Bread. Whoever eats this bread will have eternal life."

By giving himself to us in Communion, Jesus wants to unite us more and more with himself and each other.

He wants to help us walk with him on the paths of love.

The following pages will help you prepare your heart to receive him.

"I am the Bread of Life," said Jesus.

Once, about five thousand people had followed Jesus into the mountains. Soon they were hungry. But there was nothing to give them.

Then Andrew noticed a child with five loaves of barley bread and two dried fish. Jesus asked Andrew to bring the child to him.

The child gladly gave everything to Jesus. With these gifts from the child, Jesus did a wonderful thing!

He took the loaves of bread, gave thanks to God, and his friends handed them out to the crowd. He did the same with the fish. Everyone ate as much as they wanted!

The next day, people were looking for Jesus because they wanted more bread.

But Jesus had not come to give the bread of the Earth. So, he said to them:

Give us more bread...

God's bread comes down from heaven and gives life to the world. I am the Living Bread, come down from heaven. All those who eat this bread will have eternal life. I will raise them on the last day.

- If you had been that child, what would you have said to Jesus?
- Colour in the pictures while you speak to Jesus with all your heart.

52

We prepare for communion with Jesus

Before coming to the Lord's Table, we do two things: first, we say together the prayer Jesus taught us. Through it, we join together in praise and trust with all the children of God throughout the world. We express our desire to live in communion with God and with others.

> Our Father, who art in heaven,
> hallowed be thy name.
> Thy kingdom come,
> thy will be done
> on earth as it is in heaven.
>
> Give us this day our daily bread.
> Forgive us our trespasses
> as we forgive those who trespass against us;
> and lead us not into temptation
> but deliver us from evil.
> Amen.

Unfortunately, arguments and disagreements set us apart, and we sometimes find it hard to make peace, to reconcile.

But Jesus is there to help us, to give us peace. That is why the priest tells us:

"The peace of the Lord be with you always."

And we answer:

"And also with you."

Then we offer each other a sign of peace.

If, before you receive Communion, you remember that you hold a grudge against someone, ask Jesus to help you find forgiveness in your heart.

The only thing stopping us from being in communion with God and others is sin. The one who delivered us from sin was Jesus. That's why we pray to him, singing:

Lamb of God, who takes away the sins of the world, have mercy on us.
Lamb of God, who takes away the sins of the world, grant us peace.

Jesus is called the "Lamb of God" because he allowed himself to be led to his death like a lamb, without putting up any resistance.

Happy are those who are called to his supper!

A centurion, an officer in the Roman army, had a servant who was very dear to him. This servant became very ill. Not knowing what to do, the centurion went to Jesus.

Before we receive Communion, we speak to Jesus as the centurion did:

Lord, I am not worthy to receive you, but only say the word and I shall be healed.

Sharing our thoughts

1. Why was Jesus touched by the centurion's words?
2. Do you understand the word "faith"? Can you substitute another word you found in the story: T_____
3. What do the words "I am not worthy to receive you" mean? Why do we say that to Jesus?
4. What do we need to be healed of?

"Let the children come to me..."

There are people in your life with whom you like to share precious moments. You can confide in them your joys, your sadness, and your dreams. They are always happy to listen to you because they love you.

Jesus was always happy to be with children. Sometimes, his friends tried to stop children from coming up to him. They were afraid the children would bother him.

But Jesus would reproach his friends, for he loved children a lot. He talked with them and blessed them. And the children were happy when they were with him.

Now that you've read the story, close your eyes and do a prayer of meditation: you are next to Jesus and you are listening to him and speaking with him. What is he saying to you?

Then finish the two pictures and continue your prayer.

We go to the Lord's Table

Jesus said:

**"The Father who has life has sent me
and I live in communion with the Father.
Whoever eats this Bread will live
in communion with me.**

**I tell you these things so
that my joy will be in you."**
(John 6:57 and 15:11)

When you go to Communion, you go to your Great Friend,
the Lord Jesus, in response to his invitation.

The priest will present you with the host
and say: **"The Body of Christ."**
And you will answer: **"Amen."**

On some occasions he will also
offer you wine and say:
"The Blood of Christ."
And you will answer: **"Amen."**

This **"Amen"** will mean:
"Yes, I believe it is the Risen Christ who comes to me".

With your eyes, you will see only the bread and the wine. With your mouth, you will taste
only bread and wine. But in your heart, you will know that the Risen Christ himself has come
to you to help you live in communion with him and others.

**Lord Jesus, I come to you with trust.
Let me share in your eternal life.**

I have received the living God and my heart is filled with joy!

Often, during Communion, the congregation sings its joy and thanks.
But it is also important for us to be silent and pray in our heart for a few moments.

Look at the picture. These people have just shared the Bread of Life. They are telling Jesus of their joy, their love, and their thanks. They tell him of their sorrows, their worries and their wishes. They pray to him with confidence.

They also listen to what the Spirit of Jesus helps them understand in their hearts.

After your Communion, you too will spend precious times with Jesus. In order to start preparing yourself, write down the prayers you would like to say to Jesus:

To thank Jesus and tell him of your love:

_____

_____

_____

_____

To tell him of your trust and ask for his help:

_____

_____

_____

_____

We share the Bread of Life

To help you remember

- The sacraments are signs of love from the Lord. Receiving Communion is sharing the Bread of Life.
- When we share the Bread of Life, we are in communion with God and others.
- In giving himself to us, the Risen Jesus also gave us his Spirit to help us grow in love.

Go back to page 10 to see how this part of the Mass fits in with the other parts.

To follow Jesus more closely

- Your family is preparing a party for you. Try to find lots of opportunities to please the people around you in order to show them your gratitude.
- Speak to Jesus often during the day to tell him how much you are looking forward to receiving him in Communion.

To help you pray this week

Every night, you could reread these words of Jesus:

"I am the Bread of Life come down from Heaven. Whoever eats this Bread will have eternal life and I will raise them up on the last day." (John 6)

Repeat softly in your heart the words of Jesus that you like the most. Then tell Jesus of your desire to receive him:

"Come, Lord Jesus, come. My heart thirsts for you!"

7 We are sent to share the Good News

Some encounters we soon forget about. But other ones can change our lives!

On the Sunday after Jesus' death, two of his friends were going to Emmaus, their village.

Jesus joined them on the way, but they didn't recognize him. They thought that Jesus had left them forever.

You seem sad…

What! Don't you know what happened in Jerusalem?

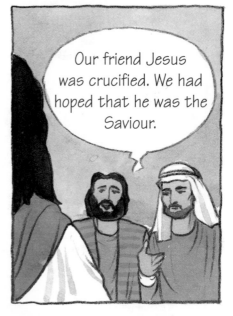

Our friend Jesus was crucified. We had hoped that he was the Saviour.

How slow you are to believe! Have you not understood the Word of God?

Jesus then explained to them that the Saviour had to suffer and die before he could rise.

The disciples listened carefully. They felt less sad, but still didn't realize the man was Jesus.

When they arrived at Emmaus, night was falling. Jesus wanted to keep going, but they invited him in.

Thank you, I will.

It's getting late, stay with us.

Sharing our thoughts

1. Why were the two disciples so sad?
2. Whom did they meet on the road?
3. Why did they want the stranger to stay with them?
4. What did Jesus do during the meal?

6. Why were they so happy?
7. Why did they return to Jerusalem?
8. How did their encounter change their lives?
9. What do you think they will try to do from then on?

We, too, have met Jesus in the Eucharist

At the end of Mass, the priest blesses us and sends us out.

Go in peace to love and serve the Lord.

Thanks be to God.

It's as if he were saying:

**"Go and share the joy of God.
Be the signs of God's love everywhere you go."**

Thank you, grandpa!

In our world,
there is happiness
and there is sadness.
Some are healthy,
others are sick.
Some are rich,
others are poor.
Some have work,
others do not.
Some have friends,
others are alone.
Some live in peace,
others are at war.

We cannot change all this
by waving a magic wand!

But Jesus does want us
to try together,
day after day,
to make things better.
At home, at school
on the playground,
everywhere,
Jesus wants us
to bring about
a little more justice,
a little more love,
a little more peace,
a little more joy.

This is what thousands of people, adults and children, try to do all over the world. And their example is catching, for they are signs of God's tender love for all the people on Earth. This is how, little by little, they help the whole human family walk along the paths of God.

This is how the Great Story of Love continues throughout the world, through each one of our lives.

Let's build a better world together

Throughout this year,
you have learned to discover
the paths of God and the joy of the Kingdom.

If you remain in communion with Jesus,
    you too can do wonderful things!

    By developing your talents and special qualities,
      by keeping your eyes and your heart open
      to the needs of others,
        by protecting our beautiful planet,
        by trying always to be an instrument of peace,
        you can make the world a better place,
        you can help the Dream of God come true.

    Then, what a beautiful life you will have!

      Sure, life will sometimes be hard.
      But you will never be alone,
    for the joy of God will always be within you.

So, if you want to continue your journey with Jesus,
    tell him so by writing down a prayer all your own
        in the space below, and have a Good Journey!

_____

_____

_____

_____

_____

**Lord,
you do wonderful
things for me.
I praise you
with all my heart!**

I, _____

have shared the Bread of Life,

for the first time,

in my Christian community

of _____

located at _____

on _____
          (day)   (month)   (year)

(sign your name)

_____

(Colour the frame.)

Memories
of a beautiful day

Here's a place for you
to put photos of your First Communion.

These are the signatures of some of the friends who celebrated this day with me.

_____

_____

_____

_____

64